#LOVESONG

This publication is made possible by the funding provided by the College of Arts and Sciences and the English Department at the University of Indianapolis. Special thanks to IngramSpark and to those who edited, designed, and published this chapbook: Rachel Holtzclaw, Rachael Neawedde, and Mirna Palacio Ornelas.

UNIVERSITY *of*
INDIANAPOLIS.

Published by Etchings Press
1400 E. Hanna Ave.
Indianapolis, Indiana 46227

etchings.uindy.edu
www.uindy.edu/cas/english

Printed by IngramSpark
ingramspark.com

Published in the United States of America

ISBN 978-0-9903475-5-2

23 22 21 20 19 18 17 2 3 4
Second Printing, 2019

Acknowledgements: Portions of this work originally appeared in *Diagram* 16.1. Portions of this work were reprinted by *Creative Nonfiction* as #cnftweets.

Credits:
All photos and even-page text: Chelsea Biondolillo
All odd-page text: Found

#LOVESONG

Chelsea Biondolillo

Dedicated
To everyone I've loved well, and a few I haven't.

Apart from other considerations, we are happiest with creatures with which we can establish some sort of communication either by vocal or gestural language... We may assume that in the distant past men and even perhaps proto-men were able to detect niceties in the utterances of birds

"Song," *The Life and Lore of the Bird*,
Edward A. Armstrong, 1975

A bird's songs and calls reveal not only its presence, but also, in many cases, its identity.

"Voice," *National Geographic Field Guide to Birds of North America*, 2011

Tell me whom you love and I'll show you who you are.

Unknown

Leather Shoe
And a Blacklist Blue
A Paintbrush
The Smell of Herbal Glue
Sunglasses
Eyelashes
Chelsea's Shoe With a Hole
And A Hole in my Heart

N, 1991

Of course I love you, too.

Chelsea–
you totally give me heart palpitations in a good way!
Thank you for your complete awesomeness as a person.
I am so stoked to be your valentine.

J, 2010

We take turns tracing one another's scars,
filling in the skin-thin cracks in our stories.
I kiss his knuckle, he my knee.

You make me smile
and you make me hurt inside
You make me Jealous
When I kiss your soft lips

And it's you
that makes me feel alive
Chelsea, I love you

S, 1990

He placed bluefin toro slices on my tongue. He slurped mussels from my spoon. We ordered different soups and splashed between the bowls.

Oh sweetie you have such cute toes…My dick is hard
tyvm

Y, 2009

You've climbed mountains, can pick fine wines, but I first loved you sick. When you came to me, my couch, my blankets, to sleep.

I'm glad I met you Chelsea,
You've shown me how good it can be,
I love you always.

A, 1992

His arms, the fine hair over the dipped plane of his sternum, his eyelids, the goosebumps that bloomed across his belly, that softest skin just behind his ankle bone; cities and nations and continents I rediscovered nightly.

WHAT ELSE? DID I MENTION I MISS YOU, BEAUTIFUL? BUT YOU KNEW THAT ALREADY.

D, 1995

We came in like a year of Marches, all roaring and cartwheels and stormy weather. But summer came back, too. We melted first, then seared at our edges.

I'm quite fond of you. I'm not very good at this sort of thing.

B, 2014

He wanted me to like *Eraserhead* and *Spinal Tap*, equally. I preferred his eyes and hands, disproportionately.

I love you, honey.

D, 2015

"It's not because I love you," I say to the empty room, practicing. "It's just that winter is long and you tell a good story."

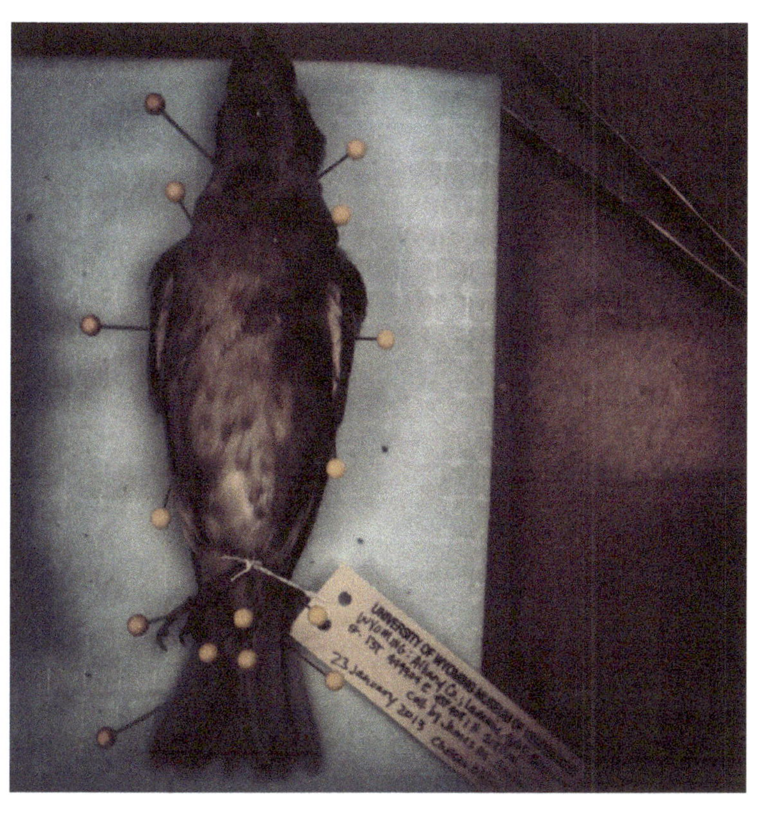

Chels…
They can tear down the place, but the memories still exist.
Love in the Past,

S, 2005

Remember painting one another with
mud at the hot springs? Remember that
horror movie moment just before the
uranium mine? Remember how badly
I behaved? How gracious you were,
anyway?

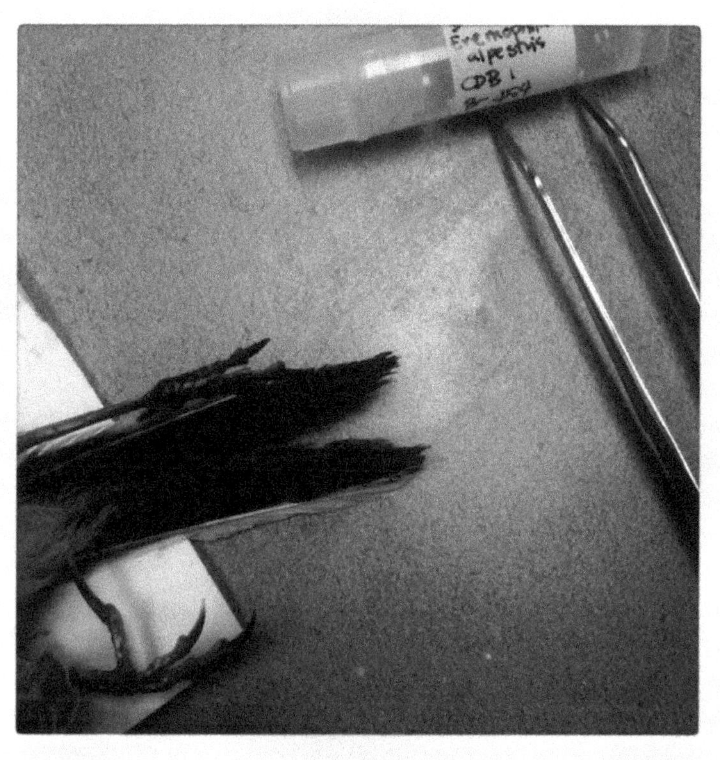

<3 –
I LONG TO TOUCH YOUR SOUL
TO TASTE THE SACREDNESS THAT IS YOU
A LOVE SO PURE, SUBLIME, SERENE
A DREAM, CONTEMPTUOUS OF TIME
COME TO ME, LOVE, AND WRAP ME UP
IN ENDLESS DREAMS, CARESSES SWEET
WITH GENTLENESS AND JOY

A, 2000

His ex-wife, that precious wood floor, the two dead cats. All these flags, waving in the wind, and I guess I thought it meant a parade.

My C
I love you intensely! I hope you are having an awesome day because everyday for me, with you in my life, is truly beautiful and wonderful.

A, 2004

Your skin was a life boat. Your slick and
toothy mouth, a barnacle on my sea-
soaked hip.

there are no words to describe how i missed thee

G, 2009

"Broken men are easier to leave later," I answered.

Though he hadn't asked.

I think your beatiful. Will you go out with me?

P, 1986

A love story: I thought he saw steel in
my stubborn backbone and admired it;
instead he saw valuable wood and readied
an axe.

I like the winter. The shear disposition of perseverance is exhilarating. I know it's morose but I try to be honest with myself. I assume things are well, although I don't think we're really in a "how's life" sorta place yet.

G, 2011

It doesn't do any good to remember the exact smoothness of your shoulder; but it snowed last night and my room is cold.

Youre the woman in my life again
I, standing at respectful attention
and listening with a gauntness of distraction
even to the scilence exchanged.

J, 1992

Yesterday one red-tailed hawk spun and called; today, two circle, quiet. Sometimes peace is just this easy, just this hard.

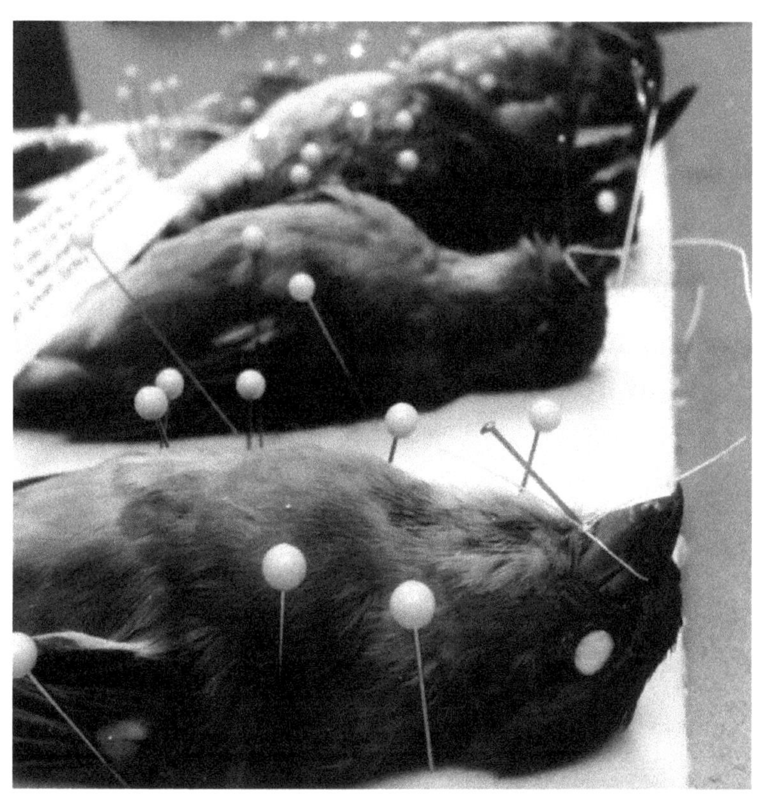

HI SWEETHEART,
I'M AT THE RODEO, ONBREAK, AND TIRED AS HELL! I MISS YOU. IT'S BEEN ABOUT A WEEK AND A HALF SINCE I'VE SEEN YOU AND I'M COUNTING THE DAYS TIL FRI. & SAT. WE'LL HAVE TO MAKE UP FOR LOST TIME.

M, 1991

About the Author

Chelsea Biondolillo is the author of the prose chapbook, *Ologies*. Her work has appeared in *Orion, Passages North, New Ohio Review, Brevity, Sonora Review, River Teeth*, and others. Her essays have been anthologized in *Best American Science and Nature Writing* (2016) and *Waveform: Twenty-first Century Essays by Women*. She is a former Olive B. O'Connor fellow and Hedgebrook resident, and she received her MFA in creative writing and environmental studies from the University of Wyoming.

About Etchings Press

Etchings Press is a student-run publisher at the University of Indianapolis that runs a post-publication award, the Whirling Prize, and contests for chapbooks and a novella. The two winners in the chapbook categories of poetry and prose (fiction or nonfiction) receive a $200 honorarium and 15 copies of the published chapbook. The winner in the novella category receives a $400 honorarium and 15 copies of the published novella.

Previous winners and publications:
Some Animals by Kelli Allen, 2016, poetry
Followers by Adam Fleming Petty, 2016 novella
Pathetic by Shannon McLeod, 2016, prose (essays)
Velocity of Slugs by Joey Connelly, 2015, poetry
Ologies by Chelsea Biondolillo, 2015, prose (essays)
Action at a Distance by Christopher Petruccelli, 2014, poetry
Static: Stories by Frederick Pelzer, 2014, prose (fiction)

For more information, please visit etchings.uindy.edu.

www.ingramcontent.com/pod-product-compliance
Lightning Source LLC
Chambersburg PA
CBHW042035120726
47911CB00027B/744